NEW FRONTIERS
EXPLORATION IN THE 20th CENTURY
THE WORLD'S OCEANS
CASS R. SANDAK

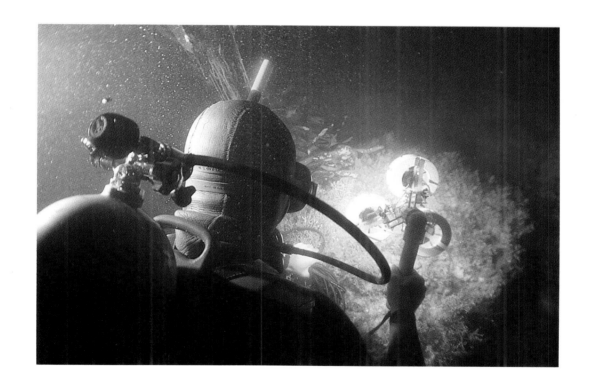

FRANKLIN WATTS
NEW YORK LONDON TORONTO SYDNEY

FOR JOY

First published in the USA
by Franklin Watts, Inc.
387 Park Avenue South
New York, N.Y. 10016

First published in 1987 by
Franklin Watts
12a Golden Square
London W1R 4BA

First published in Australia
by Franklin Watts
Australia
14 Mars Road
Lane Cove, NSW 2066

US ISBN: 0-531-10138-X
UK ISBN: 0-86313 471 8
Library of Congress
Catalog Card Number: 86-50391

Designed by Michael Cooper

TABLE OF CONTENTS

THE REALM OF THE SEAS

There are four oceans—the Atlantic, Pacific, Arctic and Indian oceans. Sometimes individual parts of these oceans are identified as seas. Four basins—huge hollows in the Earth's outer layer, or crust—hold the waters of the oceans. The Atlantic Ocean has most often been the focus of study. It was the first ocean recognized by the ancients and the first to be explored in detail.

Explorers sailed on the ocean's surface for many centuries and found new trade routes and discovered new lands and peoples. The need for improved navigation information first prompted mapmakers and early scientists to collect information about the seas—their outlines, tides, currents and surface features.

Ocean exploration in the twentieth century is a story of pioneers who have explored with a spirit of adventure and inquiry, using the most up-to-date techniques of modern science. Much of our knowledge of the seas has been amassed very recently. Even today the oceans include the least-known portions of the Earth.

The study of the ocean is called oceanography. Some oceanographers describe and classify the distribution of marine organisms. Marine scientists collect undersea specimens to be studied back in the lab, but they also observe the interactions of marine animals and plants in their natural environments. They study the origin of life in the seas, look at the chemical properties of sea water, measure the penetration of light under the sea and monitor the temperature of sea water at different locations and depths.

Physical oceanography defines and describes the geological and geographical features of oceans. The oceans are a world of constant motion. The contours of the ocean floor affect the movement of the ocean's waters by currents, and scientists study the paths of these currents.

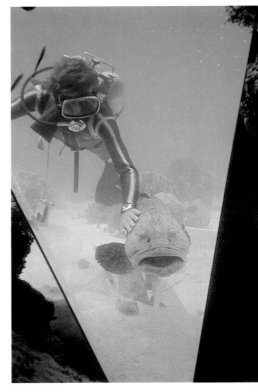

A marine biologist studies life forms near the bottom of relatively shallow coastal waters. Ocean temperatures range from about 26°C (80°F) to freezing.

The oceans cover about 70 percent of the Earth's surface. There is so much water on Earth that when seen from outer space it has been called the "Blue Planet." Although the oceans are closer to us than outer space, they are still almost as unknown.

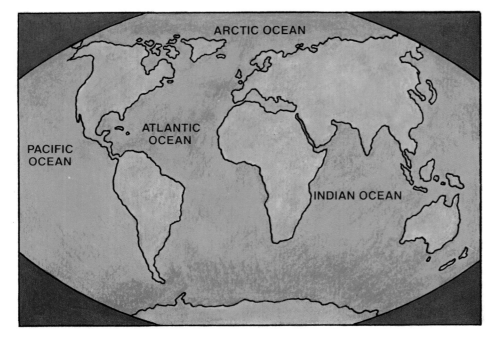

Over and under the surface of the ocean. The oceans represent only one one-thousandth of the volume of the Earth, but they hold 98.4 percent of the Earth's water. Above: The Atlantic Ocean pounds against the coast of Nova Scotia. The Atlantic Ocean has more miles of shoreline than the Pacific and Indian Oceans combined. Below: A sub-surface platform serves as a launching pad for research submersibles.

One of the most exciting developments of twentieth century exploration has been the plotting of the land under the world's oceans: the mountains, valleys and canyons that make up the oceans' unseen profile. Chemical oceanography is the study of the content and composition of sea water past and present. At least sixty-one elements occur in measurable amounts in sea water. The salt and other minerals in the sea come from the weathering and erosion of the Earth's crust. All oceanographers are concerned about pollution of the oceans and the presence of radioactive materials in them.

Scientists and engineers continue to solve the problems of undersea exploration. Two major difficulties are lack of air and the extreme pressure underwater. Because of these factors, exploration of the sea was restricted to shallow areas until recently. But new equipment has brought virtually the entire undersea world within reach. And scientists have learned to send cameras and other instruments to explore places where they themselves cannot go. Today oceanographers divide their time between the sea, the laboratory and the computer terminal. Many phases of research overlap and work together.

EARLY OCEANOGRAPHY

The story of modern oceanography begins in the 1850s. Matthew Maury (1806–73), an American hydrographer and naval officer, made daily record keeping the basis for his navigational charts. Maury's wind and current charts were the best of their time and cut sailing times on many Atlantic routes. His book, *Physical Geography of the Sea*, published in 1855, was the first work of modern oceanography. He viewed oceanography as a combination of many different sciences.

Curiosity about the undiscovered ocean world prompted the British Navy and the Royal Society to launch the *Challenger* expedition of 1872–76. The *Challenger* was a converted sail and steam warship that weighed 2,091 metric tons (2,306 tons). The ship followed Maury's wind and current charts on its expedition around the world. It was the first expedition to explore the ocean in great detail, and research from the voyage became the foundation of modern oceanography.

The *Challenger* sailed from Portsmouth, England, around Africa to the Indian Ocean and on across the Pacific. It was the first steamship to cross the Antarctic Circle. The expedition took deep soundings and discovered what we now call the Challenger Deep in the Marianas Trench, off the Marianas Islands in the Pacific. Their deepest sounding was 8,200 m (26,900 ft). The expedition made records of ocean temperatures, currents and tides.

Many facts were discovered about the oceans' depths and the contours of the sea beds. The ship carried floating laboratories for scientists. Many thousands of specimens of animal and plant life were collected, including four thousand specimens of plankton—microscopic plants and animals. Specimens were collected with "butterfly nets" of fine silk mesh. The *Challenger*'s naturalists recognized plankton as the building block of the ocean's food chain.

Dredging and sounding arrangements on board the *Challenger*. Studies of the layers of sediments on the ocean's floor help scientists create an accurate picture of the Earth, the oceans and the atmosphere in the past.

The British survey ship, HMS *Challenger*, 4,800 km (3,000 mi) southeast of the Cape of Good Hope in 1874. From December 1872 to May 1876 the ship covered 112,000 km (70,000 mi) in an around-the-world expedition. The written reports of the trip filled fifty volumes and took twenty years to complete.

Two decades later, the Norwegian naturalist Fridtjof Nansen (1861–1930) developed many of the methods used by early oceanographers. One of his inventions was the Nansen bottle, a bronze collecting tube with plugs at both ends. In 1893–96, Nansen allowed his specially reinforced ship, the *Fram*, to freeze in the polar ice to demonstrate the drift of the Arctic ice cap. He proved that the Arctic was an ocean without significant land masses.

In 1910 the Norwegian Johan Hjort led the *Michael Sars* expedition in the North Atlantic, which also involved the Canadian oceanographer Sir John Murray. Between the *Challenger* and the *Michael Sars* expeditions, at least six thousand deep-sea dredges and trawls were made, mostly in the Atlantic. Trawling and dredging are methods of collecting oceanographic samples by towing a netlike device behind a moving ship. Dredging collects samples from the sea floor. Trawling at mid-water depths can gather samples of fish or plant life.

Sir Alister Hardy led the British *Discovery I* expedition in 1925. It sailed to the South Atlantic and investigated the area near the Falkland Islands. Marine scientists on board studied whales and plankton and the environment that supports this basic link in the ocean's food chain. *Discovery II* sailed to the Antarctic in 1929–30 and continued the study of oceanic life forms and climate.

Above left. **Scientists measure the sun. Nansen's ship, the *Fram*, is in the background. Temperature readings at different ocean depths as well as other observations were recorded at least every four hours.** Above. **Water sampling on a modern research ship is not unlike the work done in Nansen's time. The bottles are triggered and closed individually to take samples of ocean water at different levels. These bottles also check salt and oxygen content and temperatures at deeper levels.**

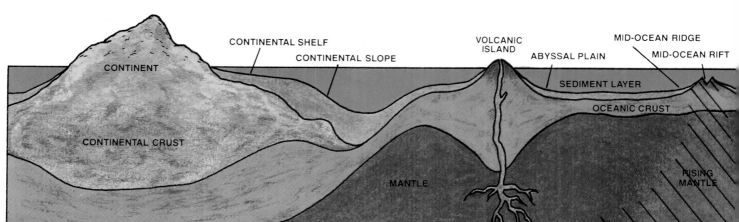

CONTINENTAL SHELF
CONTINENTAL SLOPE
CONTINENT
CONTINENTAL CRUST
VOLCANIC ISLAND
ABYSSAL PLAIN
MID-OCEAN RIDGE
MID-OCEAN RIFT
SEDIMENT LAYER
OCEANIC CRUST
MANTLE
RISING MANTLE

LEARNING MORE

Although some research had already been carried out by the beginning of the twentieth century, many questions regarding the ocean remained unanswered: What was the ocean's greatest depth? What was the nature of the ocean floor? What animals lived in the dark ocean depths and how did they survive there? Oceanographic research institutions around the world are still answering these questions today.

The real need for modern oceanographic research came during World War II. Many governments discovered that the widespread use of submarines and far-ranging weapon and surveillance systems made a thorough knowledge of the seas essential.

World War II also prompted the development of an improved echo sounder. Nickel plates vibrating in a magnetic field send pulses of ultrasonic waves downward. At intervals the echoes of the waves being received from the sea floor are converted into electric impulses. These are then recorded as dots on long rolls of paper. The sequence of dots defines a curve that shows the swells and depressions of the sea floor below.

In 1945 the Swedish oceanographer Borje Kullenberg developed the piston corer. Metal coring tubes bring up samples of the ocean floor without disturbing the layers of sediment. Cores up to 20 m (65 ft) long can be sucked up from the ocean floor by the vacuum pressure created by a piston. They are then hoisted up to be analyzed and studied. From these core samples scientists learn about the composition of the ocean bottom. Long core samples are divided into smaller sections. The samples are then placed in cold storage until they can be examined in detail.

At about the same time, American professor Harold Urey developed a method for studying the Earth's climate in past ages by measuring levels of radioactive isotopes in sediment samples.

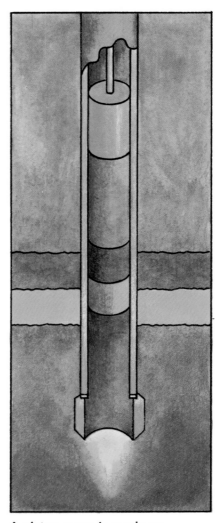

A piston corer is made up of a metal tube and a piston inside the tube. When the corer reaches the seabed, the piston stops, but the tube keeps on going. There it picks up a sample of ocean floor, which can be kept for investigation.

Modern-day core sampling. Scientists are putting geological equipment over the side of their research vessel to test sediments. If the history of the Earth is to be better known, it is essential to look to the undisturbed layers of sediments under the oceans.

Underwater sonar equipment is tested on the fantail of the USS *Valdez.* Changes in water temperature affect the speed of sound far more than changes of air temperature.

Echo sounding takes a fraction of the time needed for older, steel-wire soundings that took hours for a single measurement. Sound travels about 1,500 m (5,000 ft) per second in water. It takes only about 14 seconds for sound to bounce back from the Challenger Deep.

From 1947 to 1948 the *Albatross* and the Swedish Deep Sea expedition, under the command of Hans Pettersson, studied the Atlantic ocean bed and dredged samples as deep as 8,077 m (26,500 ft). In the Tyrrhenian Sea, an arm of the Mediterranean next to Italy, the researchers found layers of volcanic ash from eruptions of Mount Vesuvius dating back thousands of years.

In 1947 Maurice Ewing of Lamont-Doherty Geological Observatory of Columbia University began a systematic mapping of the topography of the sea floor of the North Atlantic. Before accurate soundings were taken, scientists had assumed for centuries that the sea floor was relatively flat. Now they found striking peaks and valleys. Ewing found a vast plain in the deepest part of the Atlantic. This so-called abyssal plain is more than 320 km (200 mi) wide and several hundred miles long.

In the course of mapping the sea floor, Ewing and his assistants came up with an accurate picture of the ocean's topography using data from the German *Meteor* expedition. The oceanographers on that expedition measured water temperature, plotted ocean currents and took soundings to measure the ocean's depth. Their data also showed that a mountainous ridge seemed to pass through the middle of the Atlantic floor. This ridge turned out to be the Mid-Ocean Ridge, part of an underwater mountain chain which extends more than 73,000 km (47,000 mi) around the globe. Ewing's team also discovered the Mid-Ocean Rift Valley which occurs in the middle of the Ridge chain.

The Mid-Ocean Rift is a series of cracks 13 to 48 km (8 to 30 mi) wide and in places more than a mile deep. Molten rock from inside the Earth works up through these cracks. This split in the Mid-Ocean Ridge may be a key to such diverse phenomena as the origin of Earth's mountains, and the source of earthquakes and volcanic eruptions. Here scientists can formulate and confirm the theories of sea floor spreading, plate tectonics and continental drift.

Between 1950 and 1957 Scripps Institution made over 300,000 soundings and put together a composite map of the Pacific floor. Scientists were helping to create a comprehensive picture of how forces on land and under the sea interact to change and shape the planet.

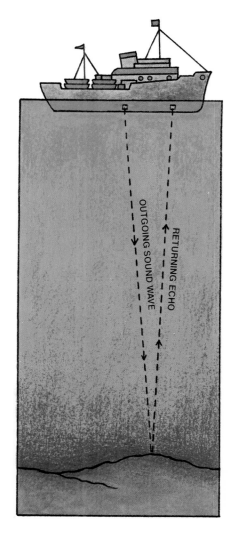

OUTGOING SOUND WAVE

RETURNING ECHO

MODERN OCEANOGRAPHY

In 1957–58 scientists around the world proclaimed the International Geophysical Year (IGY), when scientists from many nations pooled their talents and resources to increase global knowledge of the Earth.

One of the first follow-up studies on knowledge gained during the IGY was Project Mohole, named after the Mohorovicic Discontinuity, or "Moho." This is a thin layer where the Earth's crust and mantle meet, named for the Yugoslav scientist who discovered it, Andriya Mohorovicic.

The Earth's crust is the layer of soil and rock that includes the Earth's surface. It extends down to a maximum depth of about 40 km (25 mi), but is much thinner under the oceans. The seabed is therefore a good place to drill down to the Moho layer. The mantle is a thicker and deeper layer of rock that surrounds the Earth's molten core.

In the late 1960s scientists again collaborated on an ambitious undertaking called the Deep Sea Drilling Project, sponsored by America's National Science Foundation. Scientists aboard the *Glomar Challenger*, a specially built 122-m (400-ft) research vessel with a 43-m (142-ft) derrick amidships, worked in water up to 6,100 m (20,000 ft) deep and drilled for core samples 762 m (2,500 ft) beneath the ocean floor.

In 1968 the Deep Sea Drilling Project began to yield data that support the modern theories of sea floor spreading and continental drift. The evidence also supports the theory of ancient Pangaea— a single huge continent that broke up about 200 million years ago to form the continents we know today.

By analyzing data from thousands of separate soundings and studies, researchers have been able to piece together an accurate picture of the oceans. The ocean floor varies from location to location, and recent evidence shows that it is constantly expanding, pushing the continents further apart. The sea floor moves about 2.5 to 15 cm (1 to 6 in) each year.

The "FLIP" ship. Workers stand on the bow of the ship in its vertical position. The floating instrument platform is equipped for underwater viewing.

This map shows the contours of the ocean floor in the North Atlantic and is typical of the pioneer ocean-floor map work carried out by the Lamont-Doherty Geological Observatory in the fifties and sixties.

Scientists were able to drill through only 180 m (600 ft) of sediment and rock before money ran out on Project Mohole. The Earth's crust was never pierced, but the project proved that new deep-water drilling techniques could work.

The gradually sloping continental shelf extends beyond the shore and shallows. This portion of the ocean is generally less than 180 m (600 ft) deep and is well bathed in light that allows abundant plant and animal life. The ocean floor then drops off at varying distances from the shore to the colder and darker abyssal regions—the ocean deeps—and descends to terrain that is almost as varied as the surface of the continents.

The continental shelf of the Atlantic Ocean extends about 64 to 96 km (40 to 60 mi) into the sea from the water's edge. The continental shelf of the Pacific is only about 16 km (10 mi) wide. Where the continental shelf ends, the steeper continental slope begins. The slope drops at a rate of 30 to 60 m (100 to 200 ft) per mile and forms the walls of the ocean basin.

The *Glomar Challenger* was staffed by scientists from five oceanographic institutions. Researchers studied ocean sediments by drilling for core samples.

GOING DOWN

Protection was one of the first things people needed when they decided to go underwater. The earliest divers had nothing to help them as they searched shallow waters for pearls, sponges and even sunken treasure. In the early 1800s divers began to wear armored diving suits to descend to depths of 45.7 m (150 ft) and more. An even older pigskin diving suit has been found and preserved in Finland. In 1844 the French scientist Henri Milne-Edwards made one of the first research dives.

Around 1820 the German-born Augustus Siebe designed the first safely pressurized diving suit. With only slight modifications, these same suits have remained in general use for over a hundred years. Workers in shallow harbor waters still wear them. In the 1860s improved breathing equipment enabled divers to go farther down.

Divers face many problems. Decompression sickness, called "the bends," is one of the most serious. Gases that are dissolved in the blood form tiny bubbles in the blood vessels and in tissues. These bubbles can cause pain and even death. To prevent this from occurring divers must ascend to the surface in gradual stages. Decompression chambers can help the body to adjust to the changing air pressure near the surface. "Rapture of the deep" is a mental condition similar to drunkenness. Experts believe that it is caused by nitrogen or carbon dioxide in body tissues at high pressures.

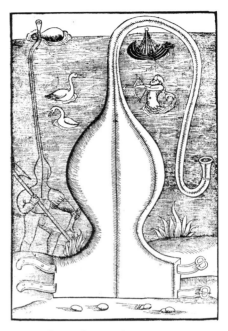

One of the first published designs for a diving helmet. From a book published in Venice, Italy, in 1553.

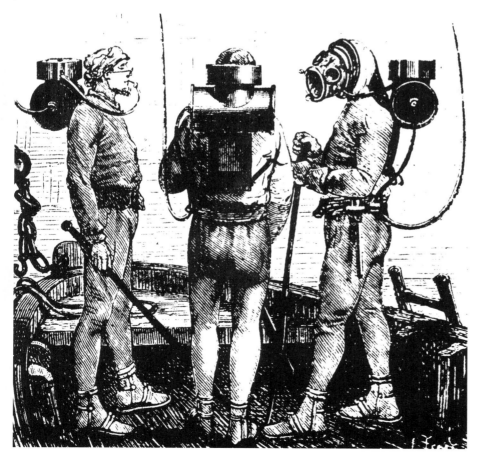

The first air regulator was developed in 1865 by the French. A pump kept the tanks on each diver's back filled with air.

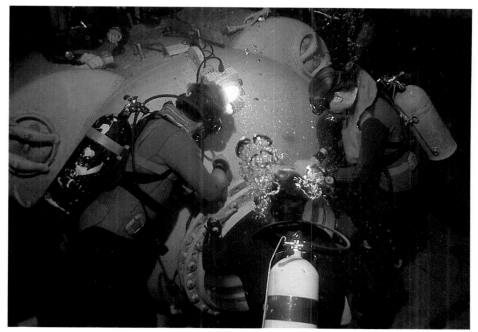

The Jim suit, named for an early test diver, Jim Jarratt, was pioneered around 1930. With only small changes it is still in common use today. The Jim suit allows divers to go to depths of about 450 m (1,500 ft), although recent dives have gone deeper. This type of suit is essential for undersea oil and gas searches. It is a diving suit that creates an artificial atmosphere that surrounds the diver and maintains normal air pressure. As a result, decompression is not needed before the diver returns to the surface. Ball and socket joints make the bulky suit more flexible. The air supply can be recycled and reprocessed for up to forty-eight hours.

The Self-Contained Underwater Breathing Apparatus (SCUBA), the modern aqualung, developed in 1943 by Emile Gagnan and Jacques Cousteau, gave divers the kind of freedom and mobility they needed and had never had before. In 1950 an improved aqualung was perfected. It enabled divers to go safely to depths of 61 m (200 ft) or less, the perfect depth for exploring the continental shelves.

The portions of the ocean floor that fringe the continents are the focus of ocean study for many researchers and divers. The continental zone encompasses the waters above the continental shelf. This relatively shallow zone of the oceans is the most accessible portion of the sea for scientists to study.

Between 60 to 90 m (200 to 300 ft) a diver equipped with only an aqualung can lose consciousness. Today's divers use masks and goggles to protect their eyes from salt water. They wear insulated rubber suits to hold in body warmth. And they put rubber fins on their feet so they can swim more efficiently.

But even the mammoth Jim suit that weighs half a ton on land is not always sufficient for undersea exploration. Because the average depth of the sea is 3,000 m (10,000 ft), and some parts are as deep as 11 km (7 mi), equipment limitations still restrict divers. Modern diving requires something more complex, even more protective.

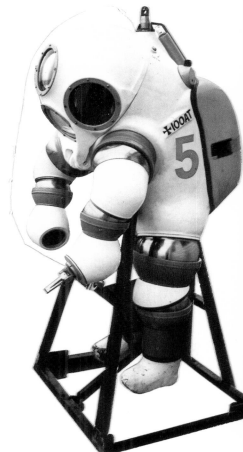

The deep-sea Jim suit is a modern version of a 1930s idea. It is used for inspection and maintenance work on undersea oil rigs, for example.

STEEL PROTECTION

Diving bells were among the world's earliest "deep-sea" vehicles. The bell shape is open to the water at the bottom, but because the air pressure is greater inside the bell, water is kept out. A hose that runs to the bell can supply air and at least some contact with people on the surface. There are many drawings of early diving bells dating back several centuries. Leonardo da Vinci even designed one. In the nineteenth and early twentieth centuries construction workers used various types of diving bells for working underwater on bridge supports.

The bathysphere was a radically new kind of apparatus. In 1926 Dr. William Beebe, an American naturalist and explorer, and Dr. Otis Barton, a geologist and engineer, worked together on a design for a new type of diving chamber. They made use of one of the principles of physics: water presses with equal force all over the surface of a sphere. If the sphere is strong enough, it will withstand any amount of pressure.

The bathysphere was a steel ball 1.42 m (4 ft 9 in) in diameter. Two men and all their scientific equipment had to fit inside. The walls were 4 cm (1½ in) thick. The inside compartment was about 134 cm (54 in) in diameter. Three small windows were made from quartz that had been melted and fused into a very strong sheet 7.5 cm (3 in) thick.

To descend, the bathysphere, supported by a steel cable 2 cm (⅞ in) thick, was lowered over the side of a ship. The ball descended until it rested on the bottom; it could not move on its own. Barton and Beebe made the first descent in 1930, and between then and 1934 they took the vessel down many times, especially in the Caribbean.

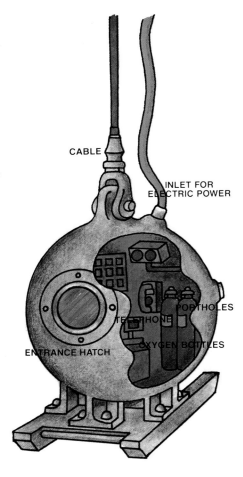

CABLE

INLET FOR ELECTRIC POWER

PORTHOLES

TELEPHONE

ENTRANCE HATCH

OXYGEN BOTTLES

William Beebe and Otis Barton, with their bathysphere, in which they descended 922 m (3,028 ft) in 1934. It was a small vessel that weighed only 2,500 kg (5,400 lb). Two oxygen tanks supplied enough air for several hours. Their deepest dive, more than half a mile, was into a world of total darkness.

On the first bathysphere descent, no photographers could be sent down, so the two men relayed their impressions to artists on the surface vessels. A telephone line maintained contact with the support crew above. The artists in turn drew their ideas of what had been described to them. On later dives, an electric searchlight allowed the two crew members to take pictures of deep-water fishes and other life forms.

In the late 1940s Auguste Piccard, a Swiss scientist, invented the bathyscaphe. He coined the name from two Greek words meaning "deep boat." Piccard had used the bathysphere and recognized its shortcomings. He wanted to develop a vessel that was faster and could be moved more easily.

The bathyscaphe is much like a bathysphere attached to a large cylindrical tank, or gondola, by heavy steel cables. Iron pellets that are used as ballast and tanks that can be flooded with water or pumped full of air or gas allow the vessel to ascend or descend, much like a balloon. The crew compartment is only 2 m (6½ ft) across, and the steel walls are 9 cm (3½ in) thick.

A later bathyscaphe was built in Italy and named the *Trieste*. In 1960 Piccard's son Jacques and a US naval lieutenant, Don Walsh, took the *Trieste* down 11 km (7 mi), setting a world's record for the deepest dive. It took about five hours for the *Trieste* to drift to the ocean's bottom and return. The dive is still the deepest that a human has ever made. The temperature 11,521 m (37,800 ft) below the surface of the sea was 38° F (2° C)—warmer than it had been at 3,657 m (12,000 ft).

In 1963 the *Trieste* investigated the site of the tragedy in which the US submarine *Thresher* and its 129 crew members were lost 2,560 m (8,400 ft) below the Atlantic.

Beebe and Barton and the Piccards were all researchers who worked with direct observation of the ocean depths. They were not content with second-hand evidence and wanted to see and experience the ocean's depths themselves.

Two shots of the *Trieste*. Left. **The bathyscaphe at sea in 1960. In the clear waters of the western Pacific, light could still be seen at a depth of 305 m (1,000 ft) through the *Trieste*'s portholes. Usually, however, underwater light ends at about 180 m (600 ft).** Right. **The vessel out of the water. Two people could sit in the sphere on the bottom of the ship and view the ocean's bottom.**

WITH COUSTEAU

Another such modern explorer is the French Jacques-Yves Cousteau, born in 1910. In the 1930s he was an officer in the French navy, but an accident cut short his career in aviation and he turned to diving. He is sometimes called the Father of Undersea Archaeology, particularly because of his pioneer work in exploring Mediterranean archaeological sites.

In 1950 Cousteau acquired *Calypso*, formerly a minesweeper in the US Navy, and converted it into a research vessel. In the 1950s he helped to pioneer the development of underwater TV cameras and related equipment. Underwater television cameras have now been used to study the oceans to depths of several thousand feet.

Cousteau perfected a bathyscaphe for the French in the early 1950s. In 1959 he developed the "diving saucer," a small submarine for two people that could be maneuvered easily. Built in France, the vessel weighed 3.174 metric tons (3½ tons) and had a 2.85-m (9½-foot) diameter. It could submerge to a depth of 305 m (1,000 ft) with a 24-hour oxygen supply. Between 1959 and 1964 this diving saucer made almost 125 descents into the warm waters of the Mediterranean.

In the 1960s Cousteau designed a series of underwater living experiments, closely watched by the US Navy. In *Conshelf I* through *Conshelf V*, aquanauts lived underwater for periods ranging from several days to several weeks. In 1962 in the first of his *Conshelf* projects, two of Cousteau's crew lived and worked for one week in a small chamber beneath the Mediterranean. One year later five crew members participated in *Conshelf II*. This time the men stayed for a whole month in a complex living environment where they made observations and were able to carry out experiments.

Below left. **The claustrophobic interior of Cousteau's one-man submarine.** Below. **Jacques-Yves Cousteau, about to enter his one-man submarine, off the coast of Madagascar.**

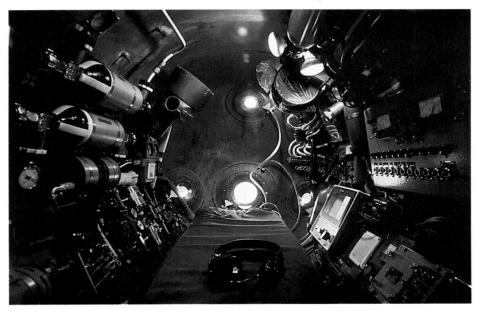

The *Conshelf II* undersea colony, almost a town in itself, was made up of the crew's cylindrical living quarters, known as "Starfish House." There was a shed for storing equipment, a hangar for launching submersible craft and "The Deep Cabin," which was the main laboratory, a fully equipped scientific center for undersea study. These *Conshelf* experiments were the first attempts at prolonged, controlled undersea living. *Conshelf III* was a success in 1965. These "voyages" have demonstrated that human beings can live and work in the ocean depths.

In 1962 Cousteau's *L'Ile Mysterieuse* (or "Mysterious Island") was established. This was a stable platform that could be anchored to the deep ocean floor. It contained a surface marine laboratory manned for sustained ocean research. From 1964 to 1970 the undersea supports for *L'Ile* were anchored in the Mediterranean at a depth of 2,621 m (8,600 ft) of water.

In 1964 Cousteau perfected a kind of diving bell with a continuous air supply that is used especially by commercial and military divers for prolonged underwater work. In 1973 he founded the Cousteau Society, dedicated to preserving the natural environment for mankind, especially the seas.

Part explorer, part inventor, part scientist, part writer, and part filmmaker, Cousteau is known as a crusader for the conservation of the seas and undersea life. Today Cousteau is world famous for his achievements and for his films on underwater exploration shown on TV around the world. In the late 1980s the renovated *Calypso* continued her career of exploration. Scientists on board were studying the relationship between water systems and the world's people.

Above left. **The Cousteau Diving Saucer.** Above. **Three men lived for twenty-three days in *Conshelf III* over 100 m (300 ft) down in the Mediterranean. They installed and operated an oil-well production unit. In this underwater photo, one of the aquanauts approaches the checkered sphere in which the men lived. Two "floaters" on the surface of the water acted as ballast and controlled the descent and ascent of the vessel, much like a submarine.**

MODERN SUBMERSIBLES

Today's submersibles are machines that can explore the world beneath the ocean's surface. Some of them carry people, but many are unmanned. A small submersible can carry one scientist and a navigator, but larger ones carry as many as five people and some can operate as much as 4,000 m (13,000 ft) below the surface. Most submersibles, manned or unmanned, are equipped with lights, cameras and mechanical arms for collecting samples. They can accommodate specialized instruments that measure the slope of the sediment surface and the temperatures of the sediments. Some submersibles are equipped with remotely operated robots that greatly extend their usefulness.

Manned submersibles are often used for commercial work, but unmanned ones are being used more and more, especially on dangerous assignments. Unmanned submersibles are used to explore the ocean bottoms and to carry out experiments. Some take photos and are even used for rescue and salvage operations. They are all attached to a support vessel or "mother" ship on the surface by means of heavy cables.

One such unmanned submersible, the *Argo*, made newspaper headlines on September 1, 1985, when it found the wreck of the giant liner *Titanic*, which collided with an iceberg and sank on April 15, 1912. A group of research scientists on board the mother ship, *Knorr*, saw what looked like metal debris and the silhouette of a ship's boiler as it flashed across a TV monitor. The wreck had been found, ending one of the most exciting searches in history.

Over the next five days the *Argo* was programmed from the *Knorr* to take many thousands of pictures of the *Titanic*. The submersible skimmed across, over and around the hull of the liner. Powerful strobe lights and video equipment made this photography possible. The *Argo* found the *Titanic* broken in two, the stern some 800 m (2,600 ft) away from the rest of the boat.

The Nemo Submersible. Two oceanographers inside are able to see what is going on while other divers work outside the vessel.

The *Alvin*, a modern submersible, is shown in 1981 in the East Pacific Rise. The *Alvin* is 6.7 m (22 ft) long and can carry a crew of three. The vessel was used in 1986 to photograph the *Titanic* and made eleven journeys down to the wreck.

In the summer of 1986 there were further trips down to explore the wreck. A new robot camera, Jason Junior (known as JJ), spent almost two weeks photographing the sunken liner. Because it was small, JJ was able to go inside the ship. Taking photographs and video film, JJ collected information about what caused the ship to sink within three hours.

Unmanned submersibles were called into the search for the remains of the Space Shuttle *Challenger* after the disaster on January 28, 1986. It was felt from the outset that the cause of the accident was a flaw in the solid rocket booster. Immediately NASA began investigating by sending sonar and robot submarines —including the Johnson Sealink and the NR-1 models— into the Atlantic Ocean off the coast of Florida to try to locate the missing pieces.

By March a flotilla of four undersea craft and ten surface vessels had located and photographed parts of the right booster as they lay scattered on the ocean floor under about 365 m (1,200 ft) of water. Costing some $20 million, the search also retrieved enough of the Shuttle's parts to substantiate the findings of NASA investigators and a presidential commission looking into the disaster.

Above left. **The *Argo*, a video camera system, found the *Titanic* in 1985.** Above. **Jason Junior leaving *Alvin* in 1986, while the submersible sits on the boat deck on the starboard side of the *Titanic*.**

A 1,800-kg (4,000-lb) piece of the Space Shuttle *Challenger*'s solid rocket booster was recovered in April 1986 with the assistance of the unmanned submersible *Gemini*, 56 km (35 mi) northeast of Cape Canaveral in almost 180 m (600 ft) of water.

RELIVING THE PAST

The oceans have always been highways of adventure. The seas have been the principal routes for commercial and military ventures throughout history. Countless shipwrecks have collected on the sea bottom over the centuries. Until recently it was almost impossible to locate or explore these wrecks. But modern technology has enabled scientists and adventurers to find and even to salvage many of the historic treasures hidden beneath the sea.

Underwater archaeology was confined to shallow waters until the aqualung made deeper diving safer and easier. In 1959 aqualung divers recovered ancient Greek and Mayan treasures. That same year an American researcher discovered thirty-five wrecks of ancient ships under one portion of the Mediterranean dating as far back as the Bronze Age.

And there are wrecks of more recent vintage. England's King Henry VIII watched in horror as the *Mary Rose,* one of Europe's first battleships, sank on July 19, 1545. The top-heavy ship sank in only 13 m (40 ft) of water in the English Channel, near Portsmouth. All but about 30 of the 700 people on board were lost.

Since the mid-1970s over five hundred divers have recovered more than seventeen thousand artifacts from the *Mary Rose* well preserved by the mud and silt of the channel. Prince Charles went down as a diver on several occasions. Wooden bows ready to be restrung and used, pieces of leather clothing and other beautifully preserved objects of everyday life were retrieved from the sunken vessel. On October 11, 1982, the remains of the hull itself were raised and brought to shore by means of a giant steel cradle and lifting frame.

In 1985 a group of salvage divers led by Mel Fisher began to recover the fabulous wealth of the Spanish ship *Atocha,* lost some three centuries before off the Florida coast. Gold, silver, jewels and historical objects worth billions were recovered. Months of patient research among shipping and navigational records led Fisher and his associates to the prize.

The kind of object being brought up by marine archaeologists: Greek amphoras dating from the third century BC found during an underwater excavation off Cyprus.

The *Mary Rose* is protected under an aluminum covering. When the ends of the canopy are sealed, the ship will be kept at 2°C and watered regularly to prevent the timbers from crumbling if they dry too quickly.

The high seas are also the proving ground for another type of historic investigation: voyages recreated to demonstrate theories about how people may have sailed from one continent to another in the past. In 1947 the Norwegian explorer Thor Heyerdahl and five others sailed the balsa raft *Kon-Tiki* 6,880 km (4,300 mi) across the Pacific Ocean from Peru on the west coast of South America to various islands in the South Seas. Carried by wind on a simple sail and by the Humboldt and South Equatorial currents, the trip took more than four months. The *Ra* expedition of 1968–69, another Heyerdahl adventure, attempted to prove that the Egyptians may have sailed to the Americas long before Columbus.

In 1976–77 the British adventurer Tim Severin sailed with nine men in an open boat from Ireland to Newfoundland recreating the voyage of Ireland's St. Brendan. In 1980 Severin then repeated the legendary seven voyages of Sinbad. His team made an Arabian dhow, based on a thousand-year-old design. Later, Severin recreated the voyages of Jason and the *Argo*.

Left: **The vessel built for Heyerdahl's *Ra* expedition.** Right. **Thor Heyerdahl on the "deck" of the *Kon-Tiki* raft in the 1940s. Both voyages demonstrated the basic seaworthiness of primitive craft.**

Under the leadership of Tim Severin, the Brendan Voyage took place in 1976-77. Ten men sailed in an 11-m (36-ft) -long open boat made from leather tanned with oak and waterproofed with lanolin in order to withstand harsh seas.

THE SEA'S LIVING THINGS

The oceans hold the key to life on our planet. Life most certainly began in the oceans. Scientists now believe the Earth is five to six billion years old. Millions of years passed before the surface of the Earth was cool enough for the waters to collect and form the oceans. But the oceans remained steaming and hot for millions of years longer. Marine sediments containing remains of algae at least 3.5 billion years old have been identified. The earliest known animal fossil is that of a jellyfish dating back one billion years.

The oceans are home to countless organisms and they are constantly revealing new life forms. Strangely, the discovery that the world at the bottom of the sea was inhabited by swarms of creatures came by accident. In 1860 a section of the transatlantic telegraph cable, which had been laid in 1858 at a depth of 1,828 m (6,000 ft), broke. When the ends of the snapped cable were brought up for repair, thousands of new kinds of plants and animals never seen before were found clinging to it.

The coelacanth is a type of lobe-finned fish thought to be similar to the type that crawled out of the seas in prehistoric times and gave rise to the vertebrates that live on land. Scientists long believed that the group of fishes had been extinct since the Mesozoic Era. However, beginning in the 1930s several specimens were discovered in the waters off Madagascar.

The ocean is divided into zones that support different types of living things. The upper layer of the ocean's water is called the pelagic zone. The greatest variety of plant and animal life occurs there. The midwater environment of the oceans is the least explored environment on Earth.

Part of the mid-ocean level is the deep scattering layer, home to many kinds of plankton that live in the shadowy depths by day. At night they move upward towards the surface in great masses to feed.

The bottom layer is called the benthic zone. Plants and animals live there on rocks or the layer of organic debris called ooze. The sponges, mussels, barnacles, oysters, clams, corals and seaweed rest on or are anchored to the seabed.

Below left. **Life on the bottom of the Pacific. This photo was taken in 1979 off the Galápagos Islands, showing animal life some 2,700 to 3,000 m (9,000 to 10,000 ft) down in the Rift Valley.**
Below. **The famous Galápagos tube worms that were discovered in 1979. Over .6 m (2 ft) long and with no mouths or stomachs, these strange creatures almost defy credibility. They indicate the existence of living things where there is no sunlight, which scientsts long believed was essential for a complete life cycle.**

Above left. **Fire coral, one of the ocean's most colorful plants, growing near High Cay in the Bahamas. It was only in 1952 that scientists conducted the first in-depth examination of coral reefs. They confirmed Darwin's theory, formulated in 1837, that coral buildup takes place on old volcano sites.** Above. **A hot-water vent deep under the surface of the ocean supports thermosynthetic life forms.**

Slow-moving and creeping animals such as lobsters, crabs, snails and certain fish such as flounder also stay near the sea bottom. Almost 90% of the ocean's creatures live on or above the continental shelves.

The ocean floor is constantly changing—sometimes very slowly, as the tectonic plates that make up the Earth's outer crust shift and renew the bottoms of the ocean basin. When hot, mineral-laden water from deep inside the Earth's crust wells up and reaches the sea floor, it shoots upward and forms chimneylike vents.

Thermosynthetic life forms have evolved near these hot springs, or sea vents. They have become oases of life for strange plant and animal forms that live in complete darkness. Scientists have recently found species of bacteria that flourish on these undersea vents. In the absence of light, these bacteria make organic compounds from water and carbon dioxide with heat energy from the hot springs. As a result, scientists have revised their thinking about the need for sunlight to support life. Research now suggests that life could have originated in the darkest depths of the sea.

Not everything in the sea is microscopic. A playful bottlenose dolphin surfaces. We have learned much about the language of dolphins from the research undertaken in recent years. Dolphins are one of the few species of living creatures that have their own form of sonar.

WORK UNDER THE SEA

In 1907 the British professor John Scott Haldane first suggested that human beings could live comfortably in twice the normal atmospheric pressure. In the 1950s and 1960s a US Navy surgeon, Captain George F. Bond, decided to test Haldane's theory when he began to plan the first habitats for the US Navy. Habitats are underwater living environments and laboratories.

Cousteau's *Conshelf I* and *Conshelf II* were the first underwater habitats. In 1964 the US Navy set up *Sealab I,* and sent four men 58.8 m (193 ft) down to live on the ocean bottom for eleven days. The sea-floor colony was designed with cameras and closed-circuit TV systems, intercoms, telephone and an ultrasonic wireless designed for use underwater. Despite the confinement, much of each day was spent outside the habitat, doing research. Support ships on the surface sent pressurized air down through hoses. If the aquanauts stay down there is no need to decompress. Only if they rise to the surface do they have to go through a gradual decompression process.

In 1966 scientists began to explore the possibilities of living for even longer periods in pressurized undersea laboratories. The US *Sealab II* was submerged to a depth of 60 m (200 ft) off the coast of California. Scott Carpenter, the second US astronaut to orbit the Earth in a space capsule, switched careers and became one of the pioneer aquanauts to take part in the 45-day *Sealab II* experiment. At the same time, Cousteau's *Conshelf III* was submerged 100 m (328 ft) off the French coast. A satellite telephone link allowed the two colonies to share and compare their findings and to talk with Gemini V astronauts orbiting 160 km (100 mi) above the Earth.

Right. **The mother ship, USS** *Florida,* **part of Project Sea-lab. The ship is connected to the research vessel** (far right) *Sealab III,* **which is then lowered down into the ocean to do on-the-spot research. There is always a tether line connecting the two vessels.**

Hydrolab, a type of undersea habitat. The diver shown here is returning home to the habitat via the special airlock chamber. The pressure inside the cabin keeps water out when the aquanaut enters.

Habitats have many objectives in common. They can extend our knowledge of undersea terrain. Marine plants and animals can be observed in their natural environment. Future ventures can be planned that will lead us to a greater realization of the ocean's gifts.

Habitats and undersea colonies point the way towards ocean resource development. Geologists now believe that many of the valuable mineral deposits found on land originate at the Mid-Ocean Rift. Here new geologic material from under the Earth's crust slowly but constantly rises up. Immediate access to these deep-lying resources may require special habitats far beneath the sea's surface. Even now habitats are being used in the search for oil, gas and sulphur deposits and to help establish fish and algae farms.

Below left. **A shark cage protects divers from the dangers of these hungry creatures. The device allows habitat divers to work in safety.** Below. **When lowered into the sea, these "telephone booths" will allow underwater divers to communicate with the support vessel.**

THE SEA FROM SPACE

Benjamin Franklin, one of the earliest oceanographers, used the technology of his time, a primitive thermometer, when he charted the Gulf Stream. This current carries warm waters from the Gulf of Mexico across the Atlantic Ocean to Europe. Today's scientists use satellites to study the seas.

Satellites provide a complete global perspective. Simultaneous data relays are able to monitor all the Earth's oceans in an instant. Signals from satellites can be stored on magnetic tape and are then analyzed by computers. These computers can make maps that show currents, eddies, and plant and temperature distributions from space. They can map currents by measuring temperature changes that send eddies plunging thousands of feet to the ocean floor.

Satellites carry infrared cameras that are able to distinguish and record slight variations in temperature of the water or in the densities of organisms. Special equipment enables color enhancement to reveal "invisible" details. Sensors exaggerate slight differences in water temperature or density. Unmanned satellites are designed to orbit so that they can maneuver over any point on the Earth's surface. Instruments fixed to buoys in the ocean below can confirm the satellite information.

Pictures showing algae concentration, plankton distribution and even fish migrations and abundance are regularly made. Satellite data can chart photosynthetic activity and show the existence and effects of pollution. Data can show coral reef and atoll formation. Weather satellites track cloud cover and patterns of motion for air masses and changes in polar ice. Satellite instruments are able to "see under" the ocean's surface electronically to measure the movement there.

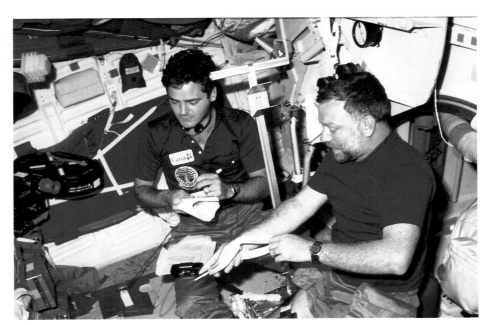

In 1984, Paul Scully-Powers became the first oceanographer to travel aboard the Space Shuttle. He is shown here (right) with Canadian payload specialist Marc Garneau. Scully-Powers spent most of his eight-day flight observing and photographing Earth's oceans.

Satellite and computer models help oceanographers understand how the atmosphere and ocean levels all the way down to the sea floor interact and affect life on our planet. The dangerous warming trend in the south Pacific off the coast of Peru, known as El Niño, is being studied and monitored from space. Shifting ocean currents upset life cycles and affect the distribution of nutrients in the sea. This periodic disruption coincides with drought and famine on land.

Scientists now know that there is a link between global weather and the movement of the seas. New studies show how energy is transferred between ocean and atmosphere. This interaction is important to understanding the source of most of our weather. Hurricanes, tidal waves, cyclones and tropical storms are studied and analyzed, and measures can be taken to prevent loss of life. Some scientists even suggest that hurricanes can be prevented by spreading a thin plastic film over superheated tropical water to keep the water from evaporating. But no one has tried it yet.

A view of weather from space. Hurricane Elena was photographed with a 70-mm camera from the Space Shuttle *Discovery* in 1985.

An appearance by El Niño in 1983 greatly upset global weather patterns. It caused droughts, famine, flooding, hurricanes and tropical storms. El Niño research is necessary because scientists believe the world is faced with the periodic return of this natural phenomenon. Here storm waves batter the California coast.

TODAY AND TOMORROW

Today's oceanographers explore the oceans in many ways. They carry out much research in laboratory tanks set up to simulate conditions under the sea. As in most scientific fields, computers are becoming more and more important as tools for marine scientists. Computers help to test new theories, especially in heat transfer and in the motion and mixing of waters with different densities, temperatures or saltiness. Computers and remotely operated mechanical devices are replacing people for much undersea exploration, especially at great depths where the work is dangerous.

Sonar and computer imaging capabilities will make the seas transparent: what scientists can't see they will be able to hear. Such devices will have tremendous impact on the future military uses of the sea. The seas will be used for secret submarine bases, for coastal defense stations and for underwater surveillance activities. Future possibilities for the seas include a network of underwater stations that will record data on conditions on the ocean floor. Scientists also foresee the use of acoustic beacons that use sound waves on the ocean bottom to guide ships on their ocean routes.

The seas are a vast potential energy source. Commercial plants in Europe use the temperature gradient in different parts of the ocean to power generators. In 1966 the first full-scale generating plant using tidal energy was established in France.

At Woods Hole Oceanographic Institution in Massachusetts, a young ecologist checks an algae tank in a closed system that changes sewage into food for oysters and is cleaned in the process.

Underwater flares developed by the US Navy will stay alight just long enough for quick inspections.

A diver about to enter a kelp forest. A kind of algae, kelp is a possible future source of food from the oceans.

A ROV (remotely operated vehicle), used for oil pipeline surveys and other underwater work in the North Sea oilfields. First used in 1984, *Solo* has a TV camera whose images are transmitted via fiber-optic cables.

A Soviet engineer has even proposed building a 73-km (46-mi)-long dam across the Bering Strait that could connect Alaska with the Soviet Union and provide energy at the same time. The dam could change temperatures in the Arctic Ocean.

Marine biological research has implications for commercial fisheries and mariculture experiments that seek to harvest the sea's wealth as a food source. The renewable resources of the sea—including algae, fish and shellfish—must be carefully managed.

Already, even in the most remote areas of the ocean, researchers like Jacques Cousteau have discovered changes in the delicate web of life in the sea. Oil spills can be destructive to fish eggs and larvae as well as birds. But the cases of cancer and genetic mutations caused by these and other pollutants may not show up for years. Should the nations allow the ocean deeps to become a dumping ground for hazardous wastes?

The future of the seas is very much the future of the human race. Unless mankind learns to conserve and preserve the natural resources of the planet, civilization is endangered. Safeguarding the ocean environment means safeguarding the quality of all life.

DATELINES

1492 Christopher Columbus sets out for India and lands in America instead.

1513 Balboa crosses from Panama and becomes the first European to see the Pacific Ocean.

1687 Isaac Newton establishes the relationship of ocean tides to the moon.

1768-76 Captain James Cook, sailing on the *Endeavour*, makes an important expedition of scientific ocean exploration.

1769 Benjamin Franklin uses temperature measurements to track the Gulf Stream, and draws up an important chart for navigators.

1855 American navigator Matthew Maury publishes the first textbook of oceanography.

1872–76 The age of modern ocean exploration begins with the *Challenger* expedition, which sails in every ocean but the Arctic.

1893–96 Fridtjof Nansen lets his ship, *Fram,* freeze in the ice in order to study the Arctic Ocean.

1910 Norwegian Johan Hjort leads *Michael Sars* expedition in the North Atlantic.

1927 Sir Hubert Wilkins takes the deepest Arctic sounding at 5,441m (17,850 ft) and later tries to travel under the North Pole in a submarine called *Nautilus.*

1934 Otis Barton and William Beebe reach a depth of 922 m (3,028 ft) near Bermuda in their bathysphere.

1945 Swedish oceanographer Borje Kullenberg develops the piston corer.

1947 Harold Urey develops system to date sediments by their oxygen isotope content.

1947 Swedish Deep Sea expedition explores Atlantic Ocean sediments.

1950 Perfection of aqualung by Cousteau allows him to explore continental shelves.

1957–58 International Geophysical Year (IGY) emphasizes scientific cooperation.

1958 US atomic submarine *Nautilus* sails under the North Pole. Another submarine, the *Skate,* surfaces at the North Pole.

1960 Jacques Piccard and Donald Walsh make their record-breaking descent to the Marianas Trench in the bathyscaphe *Trieste.*

1961 First drilling tests for Project Mohole.

1962 FLIP (Floating Instrument Platform) ship launched by Scripps Institution.

1963 *Trieste* explores wreck of the submarine *Thresher,* lost in the Atlantic.

1964 *Alvin,* a submersible capable of descents to 1,800 m (6,000 ft), is launched.

1968 *Glomar Challenger* begins its deep-sea drilling.

1985 Sunken liner *Titanic* is found by a joint US-French oceanography research team.

1986 First photos of the interior of the *Titanic* taken by robot Jason Junior.

GLOSSARY

ABYSS The portion of the ocean's basin beyond the continental slope. In general the abyss is deeper than 1,755 m (6,000 ft). Approximately 75 percent of the sea floor is abyssal plain.

ALGAE Include a large number of species of aquatic plants that vary from single celled to very complex. They contain chlorophyll, carry on photosynthesis and are the basis of the ocean's food web.

BATHYSCAPHE An ocean study vehicle consisting of a spherical compartment attached to a cylindrical steel gondola.

BATHYSPHERE A spherical steel compartment used by oceanographers to study under the ocean.

CONTINENTAL SHELF The portion of the sea floor, from water's edge at low-tide mark to a depth about 200 m (600 ft). It defines the true boundaries of the continental land masses.

CONTINENTAL SLOPE The area beyond the continental shelf that extends to the deepest parts of the oceans.

CURRENT A movement of water masses caused by winds or Earth movement, differences in water temperature or density and other natural forces.

DEEP SCATTERING LAYER A layer of water formed by concentrations of marine organisms so dense that they reflect or scatter sound waves.

ECHO SOUNDER A sound reflector used to measure the ocean depth. Also known as a depth sounder or depth reader.

FOOD CHAIN A pattern of food relationships, from the simplest to the most complex creatures.

KELP Common name for a type of algae that grows as large brown seaweed. It is a source of nutritious food additives.

KRILL Small, shrimplike crustaceans that are food for many larger animals.

MARICULTURE Sea farming, the deliberate cultivation of marine plants and animals for human consumption.

PHYTOPLANKTON Microscopic plants that inhabit the world's oceans. They are the basis of the ocean's food web and the source of most of the photosynthesis that goes on in the ocean.

PLANKTON In general, any organism (large or small) that floats or drifts in the sea and is not able to move by itself. Most plankton are microscopic.

PLATE TECTONICS The geologic study of the plates that make up the Earth's crust and the forces that cause them to float or drift over the denser mantle layer below.

RIFT A fault in the Earth's crust where material spreads away from the line of a fault. Such a rift occurs in the midst of the line of mountains known as the Mid-Ocean Range.

SEDIMENT Layers of organic and inorganic deposits built up on the sea floor over a period of time.

SONAR A system of using echos to locate underwater objects. It stands for *sound navigation and ranging*, and is found in nature in dolphins.

INDEX